Like Cats and Dogs

ALSO BY BEATRICE RICH

Children's Books

Vanessa and the Angel
Bridge House Publishing, Inc.

Vanessa and the Enchanted Painting
Bridge House Publishing, Inc.

Like Cats and Dogs

Beatrice Rich

BRIDGE HOUSE PUBLISHING, INC.

Miami

BRIDGE HOUSE PUBLISHING, INC.
3841 North East Second Avenue, 4th Floor
Miami, Florida 33137

For information about special discounts for bulk purchase,
please contact (703) 684-4057

A JANE LAHR ENTERPRISE
Designed by Patricia Fabricant

Manufactured in the United States of America

First Edition

ISBN-10: 0-9672215-3-6
ISBN-13: 978-0-9672215-3-3

Library of Congress Control Number: 2006932552

For
Fang the cat
and
Chula the dog

Foreword

STEPHEN M. SILVERMAN

Like Cats and Dogs (the book) is a little like cats and dogs (the species), in that this entertaining object you now hold in your hand is wholly unpredictable.

Just when you think this fine collection of cartoons from the even finer-pointed pen of Beatrice Rich is about to become warm and fuzzy, it leaps up and surprises you, by being sharp and—dare I say it?—biting.

"The animals I draw interact as cats and dogs might interact, but also how we, as humans, might interact," explains Rich, whose studio is located in New York's Greenwich Village, once home to many a great artist and still home to a great many dogs and cats.

"Cats and dogs are also stand-ins for our personal and social issues as humans," Rich goes on to say, even though many of us would argue that our four-legged domestic companions are actually far more discerning and certainly more sensitive than their human counterparts — as evidenced not only in real life, but in such worthy predecessors to Rich's work as James Thurber's dogs and T.S. Eliot's cats.

But don't take my word for it. (After all, nobody buys an illustrated book for its text.) Start flipping through these pages, and see if they don't give you paws.

Stephen M. Silverman's books include *David Lean; Dancing on the Ceiling: Stanley Donen and His Movies; Where There's a Will: Who Inherited What and Why*; and *Movie Mutts: Hollywood Goes to the Dogs.*

"I don't trust a cat that doesn't like chocolate!"

"He has been diagnosed with a case of Mad Hatter disease."

"He's
auditioning
for
The Sopranos."

"Don't even think about it."

"Who does
she think
she is,
Lassie?"

"I thought we were going to play fetch."

"She's in her attack mode. Act afraid."

"Forget it...
you're from the
wrong zip code."

"Everyone knows
that cats
are catty...
just ignore them."

"She's my personal shopper."

"He's doing
Tai Chi."

"Cats always
think they are
superior, and
maybe they are.
So what?!"

"I don't know
how she
does it."

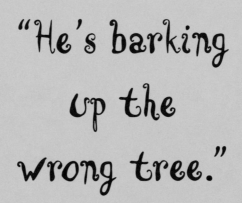

"He's barking up the wrong tree."

"Someone told
him he had
a nice voice."

"They are
from a
blue state."

"You want
to do what...
you want to
adopt a kitten?"

"I love it when you growl like that."

"She could use an extreme makeover!"

"Do you think she had a nose job?"

"You may
be able to
climb a tree,
but I can bark."

"Poor dear,
so clumsy.
He was a
dog in a
previous life."

"I see
the future...
and it is
cats."

"This is your last chance. Where did you hide my ball?"

"According to these tests, you are deficient in red wine, dark chocolate, rare steaks and ice cream."

"Tuna, salmon, sardines, mackerel... that's all he ever thinks about."

"He's conflicted. He doesn't know whether to send the bone to the Smithsonian, or bury it."

"It's his version of Palm Beach."

"He's searching for signs of intelligent cat life on other planets."

"Go to the corner, turn left, and you will come to the not-too-distant future."

"Just because she has a blond fur coat, perfect teeth, emerald green eyes, wears a gold collar and lives in a mansion, doesn't mean I am jealous."

"I can't
believe I ate
the whole thing."

"He just got his DNA report. It says he is descended from an ancient tribe of lions."

"He's depressed because he isn't a cat."

"That cat is supercilious, and super silly."